You Might Be a Redneck If®. . .

This Is the
Biggest Book
You've Ever Read

Jeff Foxworthy

Illustrations by David Boyd

RUTLEDGE HILL PRESS
Nashville, Tennessee
A Division of Thomas Nelson Publishers
Since 1798

www.thomasnelson.com

Published by Rutledge Hill Press, a Division of Thomas Nelson, Inc., P.O. Box 141000, Nashville, Tennessee 37214.

Library of Congress Cataloging-in-Publication Data

You might be a redneck if—this is the biggest book you've ever read / Jeff Foxworthy ; illustrations by David Boyd.

   p. cm.

  ISBN 1-4016-0193-6

  1. Rednecks—Humor 2. Rednecks—Caricatures and cartoons. I. Boyd, David, 1938– II. Title.

PN6231.R38F69 2004b

818'.5402—dc22   2004012465

Printed in the United States of America

05 06 07 08 — 5

Contents

Introduction

After 15 years, you'd think I would have heard every redneck joke conceivable. But hardly a day goes by that someone doesn't come up to me and say, "Hey, Jeff, here's one I betcha haven't heard." And many times they're right.

There was a point in my career when I thought it was time to move on from the redneck material. I even published a book entitled *The Final Helping of You Might Be a Redneck If . . . .* But as you can tell from the book you hold in your hands, there was still some meat on that bone.

I've often described redneckism as "a glorious absence of sophistication." Being a redneck has nothing to do with money or social standing—there are rednecks everywhere you turn. Open to almost any page of this book and you'll recognize a family member, a friend, or a coworker. It's possible you might even recognize yourself.

I once developed a scale to help readers determine what shade of red their neck might be. It went something like this:

If you identify with fewer than 5 redneck lines, you probably don't get asked out very often, and your butler probably steals from you.

6–10 means you'll probably keep this book on the back of the toilet.

11–20 means you're a regular at the state fair.

21–40 indicates I'll see you at the next family reunion.

41–75 means there's an appliance for sale in your front yard.

76–100 suggests you've seen Elvis within the past year.

101–125 means you wear an orange vest to work, for recreation, or for a night out on the town.

And if you identify with more than 126 redneck lines, somebody else read this book to you.

To all of you who have provided this material, who have laughed and loved along with me, I say, "Thank you, and may God bless."

Jeff Foxworthy

Family
Fam-v-lee

Families are proof positive that God has a sense of humor. He takes people with nothing in common except a recessive chin (Uncle Ed) or a hairy back (Aunt Jessie) and throws them together for a lifetime. You can pick your friends, but you're stuck with family.

When I first started doing redneck material as part of my stand-up routine, my mother asked, "Where on earth do you come up with that stuff?" Gee, Mom, I don't know, but have you looked around you lately? Our family has more nuts than Planters. This is from a woman who, when asked if she would like a window seat on an airplane, said, "Oh, I better not. I just had my hair done."

But any time you start worrying because your family is on speed dial at the *Jerry Springer Show,* visit a state fair almost anywhere in this great country. You'll see people who were born, raised, married, and had families without ever leaving their own property—people whose family tree does not fork! People who have reached the bottom of an all-you-can-eat buffet. People who have been turned away from yard sales. In less than five minutes you'll be saying, "You know what? We're all right. We're dang near royalty!"

You Might Be a Redneck If . . .

According to your birth certificate,
your father's name was X.

☆

You put ninth grade on hold while you started a family.

☆

Any of your relatives were buried with a flyswatter.

☆

You've ever had to haul a can of paint to the top of a
water tower to defend your sister's honor.

☆

You cried the day your son tapped his first keg.

☆

The closest you've come to royalty
is eating at Burger King.

You Might Be a Redneck If . . .

Your family
tree does
not fork.

You Might Be a Redneck If . . .

Your kids attend your high school graduation.

☆

Diners change tables when your family sits near them.

☆

Your mother taught you how to flip a cigarette.

☆

More than two of your children have been banned
for life from a day-care center.

☆

You start a fight in a bar and your wife finishes it.

☆

Most of your in-laws are outlaws.

You Might Be a Redneck If . . .

Everyone in your family is an Elvis impersonator.

Your baby's first words were "Rack 'em!"

☆

You think the theory of relativity has something to do with inbreeding.

Anyone in your family has
taken a UFO ride lately.

You Might Be a Redneck If . . .

Your brothers convinced you that you were an only child.

⭐

At the country club, you make your mother-in-law get out of the truck at the "Bag Drop" sign.

⭐

You understood everything Jodie Foster said in the movie *Nell.*

⭐

All your kids have the middle name Elvis.

⭐

Your richest relative buys a new house and you have to help take the wheels off.

⭐

The emergency-room nurse knows everyone in your family by name.

You Might Be a Redneck If . . .

All of your four-letter words are two syllables.

☆

Your grandmother has ever climbed into the ring
at a wrestling match.

☆

You and your wife have the same haircut.

☆

Beer bellies run in your family.

☆

You were born with a plastic spoon in your mouth.

☆

Your son is named for your favorite pro wrestler.

You Might Be a Redneck If . . .

Your family reunion features a chewing tobacco spit-off.

☆

You can't visit relatives without getting mud on your tires.

☆

Your grandmother has ever stopped to relieve herself
on the side of the highway.

☆

Every member of your family has been shot at.

☆

Your kid's favorite bedtime story is "Curious George
and the High-Voltage Fence."

☆

People ask you if you were in the movie *Deliverance*.

You Might Be a Redneck If . . .

Your mother keeps a spit cup on the ironing board.

You have more than two brothers named
Bubba or Junior.

☆

All your relatives would have to die to wipe out illiteracy.

You Might Be a Redneck If . . .

When you hear someone talking about "the King," you're
not sure if they're talking about Elvis or Richard Petty.

☆

Your birth was announced in *Auto Trader*.

☆

You and your wife's family reunions
are one and the same.

☆

You've ever hollered,
"You kids quit playing on that sheet metal!"

☆

The Glamour Shots people give you your money back.

☆

Your good deed for the month was hiding your
brother for a few days.

Your coat of arms features kudzu.

You Might Be a Redneck If . . .

Your family reunion was held at a skating rink.

☆

One of your relatives had his CB handle in his obituary.

☆

Your mother has more chest hair than your father.

☆

You steal the towels when you stay overnight
with relatives.

☆

The highlight of your family reunion
was your sister's nude dancing debut.

☆

Your daddy's headstone includes the words
"worthless" and "varmint."

You Might Be a Redneck If . . .

Your brother-in-law is also your uncle.

You Might Be a Redneck If . . .

The orthodontist retired when he finished
with your family.

☆

Your mother has ever been involved
in a fistfight at a high school sports event.

☆

There are big rigs named after your sister.

☆

Someone asks, "Where's your bowling bag?" and you
answer, "She's at home with the kids."

☆

You can see your bottom lip without a mirror.

☆

You think "going back to your roots" means
growing out the peroxide.

You Might Be a Redneck If . . .

Three generations of your family have been represented
in the same wet T-shirt contest.

☆

You break wind in public and blame it on your kid.

☆

You bum a dip from your mother.

☆

Your grandpappy's hearing aid is a construction cone.

☆

You don't recognize several relatives when they are sober.

☆

A full moon reminds you
of your mother-in-law pulling weeds.

You tell Grandpa he has something in his teeth, and he takes them out to see.

Your family stays cool by sitting on the porch naked.

☆

When describing your kids, you use the phrase "dumb as a brick."

You Might Be a Redneck If . . .

You know your daddy's CB handle but not his real name.

☆

Your uncle Bob died from peeing on an electric fence.

☆

Your family reunion is sponsored by a beer company.

☆

The *Jerry Springer Show* asks you back.

☆

You and your father attend the same class reunion.

☆

They call you a "soccer mom"
because the entire team is your kids.

Your father fully executes the "pull my finger" trick during Christmas dinner.

There's no record of your birth—anywhere.

☆

Your 23-channel CB radio is used to communicate with your family.

You Might Be a Redneck If . . .

You invite all your relatives over
to see your new ceiling fan.

☆

You're related to the stripper at your bachelor party.

☆

You think "neighborhood watch"
is what your mother-in-law does on the porch all day.

☆

The only thing you inherited from your father
was alcoholism.

☆

You've ever learned something about your mama
from a restroom wall.

☆

Your grandmother is pregnant.

Your dad walks you to school because you're in the same grade.

You wrap up your older children's outgrown underwear to give to your younger child for his birthday.

☆

You think four-on-the-floor is a sleeping arrangement.

You Might Be a Redneck If . . .

Your kids' school bags have
Dale Earnhardt stickers on them.

☆

The farthest anyone traveled
to your family reunion was two miles.

☆

Your wife has four-wheel drive on her vacuum cleaner.

☆

There's no cut-off age for sleeping with your parents.

☆

Your daughter's Barbie Dream House
has a clothesline in the front yard.

☆

Your wife puts candles on a pan of corn bread
for your birthday.

You Might Be a Redneck If . . .

Your uncle is better known as "the Goat Man."

☆

You went to grade school with your mother-in-law.

☆

Your father encourages you to quit school because Larry
has an opening on the lube rack.

☆

Anyone in your family has ever purchased peroxide
in a gallon container.

☆

You have to walk through a metal detector
to go to your family reunion.

☆

Your 14-year-old smokes in front of her kids.

You Might Be a Redneck If . . .

You list Dr Pepper as your family physician.

☆

You send your kid in for treatment because you think
he's hooked on phonics.

☆

All your cousins are kissing cousins.

☆

Your kids' trick-or-treating covered three counties.

☆

You got your nose broken at your sister's wedding.

☆

Your high school class voted you "Best Mother."

You Might Be a Redneck If . . .

Your grandmother knows how to correctly execute the "sleeper hold."

Any of your children were conceived on a tire swing.

☆

You'll answer to more than one nickname.

You Might Be a Redneck If . . .

You're constantly having to erase your sister's name
from bathroom walls.

☆

You have a cousin who no one
in the family ever talks about.

☆

Your mother owns a Lynyrd Skynyrd T-shirt.

☆

Truckers tell your wife to watch her language.

☆

You wear a giant foam finger at your child's graduation.

☆

Your gene pool doesn't have a "deep end."

Love & Marriage
Luv n' Mar-ij

Nothing changes a relationship quicker than wedding vows.

Your furniture that was "comfy" before you got married ends up on the curb faster than a woman trying to parallel park.

Your friends who were "cute" before the vows become perverts afterwards. But that shouldn't be surprising—your wife doesn't want to hear about their sexual exploits ("So there I was, tied to the Black & Decker Workmate, when she brings out the ShopVac that cleans both wet and dry . . ."), and you can no longer share your stories ("We took the phone off the hook, locked the front door, turned on the dishwasher, and then . . .").

And your manners become legendary among your wife's friends. "First time I saw Tom, he was naked on the side of the road, eating roots and kudzu with his bare hands. I took him home, taught him to wear a shirt and eat with a spoon, and later we got him a regular job."

You Might Be a Redneck If . . .

A dating service matches you up with a relative.

☆

You saved your allowance to pay for your first divorce.

☆

Your honeymoon plans included a deer camp.

☆

A woman says she's game, so you shoot her.

☆

You've ever given your date flowers you stole
from a cemetery.

☆

You tell your kids the facts of life and they interrupt you
with corrections.

You Might Be a Redneck If . . .

You proposed at Denny's.

Any of your children are the result of a conjugal visit.

You can't marry your sweetheart because there
is a law against it.

You missed sex education class because
your baby was sick.

The first time you saw your wife in lingerie,
you had to pay a cover charge.

Your wedding day began in a liquor store
and ended in a tattoo parlor.

You Might Be a Redneck If . . .

You've ever had sex in a satellite dish.

You dated your daddy's current wife in high school.

☆

The biggest compliment you got at your wedding was how cute your baby was.

You Might Be a Redneck If . . .

There were dogs in the church on your wedding day.

You request the honeymoon suite at the Motel 6.

☆

Three generations of the women in your family are currently breast-feeding.

You Might Be a Redneck If . . .

You taped WWF wrestling over your wedding video.

☆

You think a sex change means trying the backseat.

☆

When your wife left you, she took the house with her.

☆

You dump your boyfriend
because your husband has been paroled.

☆

You've ever opened a beer while making love.

☆

You're in the same grade as your second husband.

You Might Be a Redneck If . . .

You show your boyfriend you really love him by carving his name on your arm.

All your wedding photos have someone torn out of them.

☆

You gave your wife a glue gun for your anniversary.

You Might Be a Redneck If . . .

You had a marriage license
before you had a driver's license.

☆

Your sister's educational goal is to get out of high school
before she gets pregnant.

☆

The fountain at your wedding spewed beer
instead of champagne.

☆

You have visitation rights to a dog.

☆

You hit on the midwife while your wife's in labor.

☆

Your current wife was a bridesmaid at your first wedding.

You Might Be a Redneck If . . .

You think rug burns are a sexually transmitted disease.

☆

Your daddy handed out cigarettes the day you were born.

☆

You proposed to your wife through
a mouthful of Cheetos.

☆

Two of your weddings made
America's Funniest Home Videos.

☆

Your daughter mistakenly thought you'd attend her
wedding on opening day of deer season.

☆

You give your marital status as "often."

You Might Be a Redneck If . . .

WELL... IF YOU ARE, IT AINT MINE CAUSE I HAD THE 'MERGENCY BRAKE ON THE WHOLE TIME !

You practice "safe sex" by putting on the emergency brake.

Any of your wedding gifts came from an Army Navy store.

☆

You've ever reused wedding invitations.

You Might Be a Redneck If . . .

The miniature figures atop your wedding cake
included two dogs.

☆

You select a date's corsage to match her tattoo.

☆

You stand under the mistletoe at Christmas and wait
for Granny and Cousin Sue Ellen to walk by.

☆

Your wife still wears a miniskirt eight months
into pregnancy.

☆

You thought Ned Beatty was sexy in *Deliverance.*

☆

You swept up the rice at the wedding
and served it at the reception.

You Might Be a Redneck If . . .

Any of your children were conceived at a traffic signal.

HURRY UP, BABY. THE LIGHT'S CHANGING!

You said your wedding vows while watching a football game out of the corner of your eye.

☆

You learned the facts of life by watching dogs.

Your sister is the third generation of women in your family to conceive a baby because of an alien abduction.

You whistle at women in church.

☆

You've ever told a bride, "You clean up pretty good."

You Might Be a Redneck If . . .

You took your honeymoon photos to show-and-tell.

☆

Your first wife has been on six talk shows
talking about you.

☆

The last thing your ex-wife said to you was
"It's me or them dogs."

☆

You put "horns" on your new bride
in your wedding pictures.

☆

You use your daughter's wedding as an excuse
to buy a new shotgun.

☆

You view the upcoming family reunion as a chance
to meet women.

You Might Be a Redneck If . . .

You've ever lost your wife in a poker game.

You asked the preacher to repeat the question
during your wedding vows.

☆

You've been married three times
and still have the same in-laws.

You Might Be a Redneck If . . .

You had a prom night and a wedding night,
but not in that order.

☆

You refer to the church where you were married
as "the scene of the crime."

☆

Your tattoo of Elvis was supposed
to be a portrait of your wife.

☆

At your wedding reception you put Alka-Seltzer
in cheap wine to get "champagne."

☆

You were registered at the Everything's a Dollar store.

☆

You won your wife's wedding ring by knocking down
three milk bottles with a baseball.

You Might Be a Redneck If . . .

Your prenuptial agreement mentions chickens.

☆

You think disposable diapers
are an appropriate wedding gift.

☆

Any of your daughters are older than your wife.

☆

Your keepsake from prom night came nine months later
and weighed seven pounds, three ounces.

☆

You're making payments on more than one wedding ring.

☆

Your own mother testified against you in divorce court.

You Might Be a Redneck If . . .

Any of your children were conceived in a car wash.

Winn-Dixie catered your wedding.

☆

At least one dog slept in your bed on your wedding night.

You Might Be a Redneck If . . .

After making love, you have to ask your date
to roll down the window.

The flowers in your bridal bouquet were plastic.

You met your last three wives while on the pay phone
outside the convenience store.

You've ever French-kissed within five feet of a Dumpster.

During your wedding, when you kissed the bride,
your John Deere hat fell off.

You've ever had to move a baby seat to make love.

You Might Be a Redneck If . . .

Your wedding music was played on a banjo.

Your most romantic moment happened at a drive-thru.

☆

You met your wife through the personal ads in
Bowhunter magazine.

You Might Be a Redneck If . . .

Your wedding invitations say, "Same time, same place."

☆

Tires were featured in your divorce settlement.

☆

Your rehearsal dinner was at Hooters.

☆

You signed your marriage license on the hood of a car.

☆

Your wedding cake was made by Sara Lee.

☆

Your will states your wife can't touch your money
until she's 14.

Your wedding dress was a leopard-skin print.

You Might Be a Redneck If . . .

You proposed to your wife while working
under your truck.

☆

You've ever been to a wedding reception
at the Waffle House.

☆

The first time you danced with your wife, it cost you $20.

☆

You've ever given a full set of NASCAR plastic cups as a
wedding present.

☆

For laughs, you watch your wife's delivery video
backwards.

☆

You've ever been asked, "Daddy,
why don't you marry Mommy?"

Wheels

Weelz

When I got a paying job, I just had to have a two-tone Rally Sport Camaro. I couldn't help myself—it's genetic. So I bought the car, added enough stereo equipment to rattle the windows (of the car next to me), and immediately fell behind in the payments.

One night at about six'clock, a guy from the finance company showed up at my door. "Mr. Foxworthy, I've come to get your car. You haven't made a payment in three months. Unless you can give me $500 right now, the Camaro's going with me."

I said, "Five hundred bucks? Who keeps that kind of cash on them?"

"Well," he said, "I can take a check."

"A check? Sure, I can write you a check," I boasted. "I thought you meant real money."

So I wrote him a rubber check and hid the car in a friend's garage until I got caught up on the payments. Like I said, it's genetic.

You Might Be a Redneck If . . .

You painted your truck camouflage
and now you can't find it.

☆

Your car doesn't leak oil—it's just marking its territory.

☆

After removing the empty beer cans from your car,
you find you get 15 more miles per gallon.

☆

You can breast-feed while driving a stick shift.

☆

Auto salvage yards regard you as competition.

☆

You've sent fan mail to a monster truck.

You Might Be a Redneck If . . .

You slam the door on your truck and your shotgun creates an instant sunroof.

Getting your car inspected means paying a bribe.

☆

Your house doesn't have curtains but your truck does.

You Might Be a Redneck If . . .

Your bumper sticker says,
"My child whipped your honor student's ass."

Ⓧ

You've ever moved furniture in a horse trailer.

Ⓧ

You always have to sign a release at the car wash.

Ⓧ

The travel trailer you were pulling passes you
on the highway.

Ⓧ

You blow your nose and check your oil
using the same rag.

Ⓧ

You've ever put a racecar on a prayer list.

You Might Be a Redneck If . . .

You've ever gift wrapped a tire.

Everything you won at the fair is hanging from your rearview mirror.

☆

You can identify your friends by the sounds of their mufflers.

You Might Be a Redneck If . . .

Your idea of a traffic jam is being the second car
at the traffic light.

☆

You can count the highway stripes
through your floorboard.

☆

You drive 600 miles to see an image of Elvis
that has miraculously appeared in water stains
on the ceiling of a trailer.

☆

Mechanics ask you to sit down before giving an estimate
on your car.

☆

You have a set of "monster mudder" tires
on your station wagon.

☆

You own eight cars but still have to bum a ride to work.

You Might Be a Redneck If . . .

You've ever hit a bump in the road and lost half of your worldly possessions.

You know how to fit three baby seats into the back of a Trans Am.

☆

Your truck, car, boat, and mower all share the same battery.

You Might Be a Redneck If . . .

Your riding lawn mower has cup holders.

☆

You park in handicapped spaces based
on your SAT score.

☆

You can give the date and place
of every bullet hole in your car.

☆

Your truck can pass over a 55-gallon drum
without touching it.

☆

Everyone who sees your car asks,
"What happened to the paint?"

☆

Your bicycle has a gun rack.

You Might Be a Redneck If . . .

You have more CBs than CDs.

You've ever made a Christmas wreath out of a tire.

Every car you own is permanently for sale.

You make a car payment on time and the bank calls
to see if you are okay.

Your best watch came free with 10 gallons of gas.

Your biggest childhood memory is standing
by the road while Dad worked on the truck.

You've ever written Richard Petty's name on a presidential ballot.

Hitchhikers won't get in the car with you.

☆

You hold the hood of your car open with your head while you work on it.

You Might Be a Redneck If . . .

Your car stereo costs more than your car.

☆

None of the tires on your van are the same size.

☆

You've ever changed your baby on the hood of a car.

☆

Your wife thinks your car is a "CH V O ET."

☆

Your car breaks down on the side
of the road and you never go back and get it.

☆

You own half of a pickup truck.

You Might Be a Redneck If . . .

You taught your wife to drive so you would have a way home from parties.

You clean your garage and find a motorcycle.

☆

It's impossible to pick up your key chain
with just one hand.

You Might Be a Redneck If . . .

You have a bumper sticker that says,
"If you can read this, we're probably not related."

☆

Your car makes noises mechanics
have never heard before.

☆

You've ever listed fuzzy dice on an insurance claim.

☆

You fix holes in your truck with duct tape.

☆

After the prom, you drove the truck
while your date hit road signs with beer bottles.

☆

Your five-year-old can rebuild a carburetor.

You Might Be a Redneck If . . .

You named each of your kids after the car they were conceived in.

You've ever ridden on a luggage rack.

☆

Your front and rear license plates are handwritten on cardboard.

You Might Be a Redneck If . . .

Your idea of cruise control is putting a rock
on the gas pedal.

☆

Fewer than half the cars you own run.

☆

Your wife has ever said,
"Come move this transmission so I can take a bath."

☆

You think your dashboard is the best place
to keep your hats.

☆

You say you're in the oil business
because you pump gas for a living.

☆

You wash your entire car with the gas station squeegee.

You Might Be a Redneck If . . .

You've ever driven a Camaro into the top of a tree.

You've ever rebuilt a motor in
a Pep Boys parking lot.

You Might Be a Redneck If . . .

Your wife's favorite perfume is New Car Smell.

☆

You think the Kremlin is the car you drove in high school.

☆

Your family car has flames painted down both sides.

☆

Local air quality plummets when you start your truck.

☆

Your daughter refuses to drive your truck because of the
"Honk if you're horny" bumper sticker.

☆

You've ever had to turn your truck around
because of bridge clearance restrictions.

You Might Be a Redneck If . . .

Blowing a tire means a new flowerpot for the front yard.

You're not actually able to read *The Richard Petty Story,* but you like looking at the pictures.

☆

You've ever cleaned your brake drums in the dishwasher.

You Might Be a Redneck If . . .

Grass is growing in the floorboards of your car.

☆

You have a four-door car,
but only one door will open and close.

☆

You keep a chainsaw in the trunk—"just in case."

☆

You still use your dead uncle's
handicapped parking sticker.

☆

You know how many bales of hay your car can hold.

☆

You believe the most effective form of advertising is on
the side of a car going 200 miles per hour . . . round and
round and round.

You Might Be a Redneck If . . .

Your CB antenna slaps stoplights
when you go through town.

☆

You could retire by recycling all the cans
in the bed of your truck.

☆

The kids are going hungry tonight because you just had
to have those Yosemite Sam mud flaps.

☆

You're driving a vehicle with no original body parts.

☆

You're listed as "uninsurable"
before you're even out of high school.

☆

You've ever done your Christmas shopping
at a truck stop.

You Might Be a Redneck If . . .

You go to a stock car race and don't need a program.

☆

You refer to your wife and mother-in-law
as "dual air bags."

☆

People driving directly behind you
become faint and dizzy.

☆

You've ever relieved yourself from a moving vehicle.

☆

Your passenger's-side window is a Hefty bag.

☆

You use speed bumps to try to get your truck airborne.

Your house has ever been
involved in a traffic accident.

Someone touches your car and has to get a tetanus shot.

☆

You've ever driven for more than a month
on a baby spare tire.

You Might Be a Redneck If . . .

Your hood ornament used to be a bowling trophy.

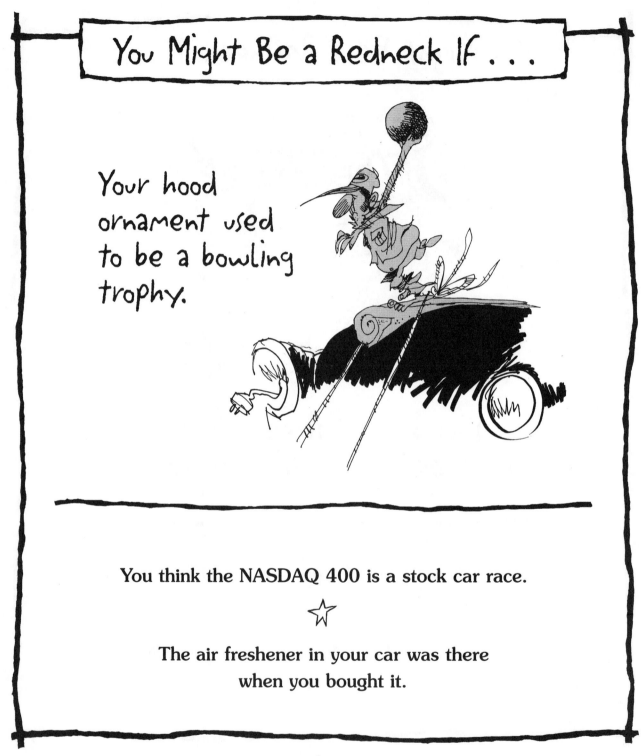

You think the NASDAQ 400 is a stock car race.

☆

The air freshener in your car was there when you bought it.

You Might Be a Redneck If . . .

The convenience store calls you
when the new *Auto Trader* arrives.

☆

Your truck has 12 bumper stickers
but no inspection stickers.

☆

Your car's horn plays "Sweet Home Alabama."

☆

You've ever had a conversation about truck tires
that lasted more than an hour.

☆

You pick your friends based
on their ownership of jumper cables.

☆

You think the last four words of the national anthem are
"Gentlemen, start your engines."

You Might Be a Redneck If . . .

You hand painted the whitewalls on your tires.

☆

Tidying your yard involves calling a tow truck.

☆

Every time you rebuild your motor,
there are a few parts left over.

☆

You think the French Riviera is a fancy Buick.

☆

You've ever had to have a wrecker pull your car out of a
pothole in your driveway.

☆

Nobody can rebuild an engine like your mama.

You Might Be a Redneck If . . .

You've sold a car to settle a bar tab.

☆

Your college graduation ceremony included parallel parking an 18-wheeler.

☆

The front license plate of your car has the words "Foxy Lady" written in airbrush.

☆

Your will mentions tires.

☆

You drive across town to see a car wreck.

☆

You've never bought a car you could drive home.

You Might Be a Redneck If . . .

The rear tires on your car
are twice as wide as the front ones.

☆

You consider the traffic sign "Merge"
as a personal challenge.

☆

You won't stop at a rest area
if you have an empty beer can in the car.

☆

You've paid for a car with quarters.

☆

There are hubcap wind chimes anywhere on your block.

☆

You spend more time under your car than in it.

You Might Be a Redneck If . . .

You paint your car with house paint.

The cigarette lighter in your car is your wife.

☆

Your definition of "getting lucky"
is passing the emissions test.

You Might Be a Redneck If . . .

You've ever passed an entire funeral procession.

☆

All of your relatives' cars have "Tag Stolen"
signs in the rear windows.

☆

Your idea of going formal is a black truck.

☆

The only signal you use while driving is "the finger."

☆

You can take your bra off while driving.

☆

You've ever ridden all the way to Florida
with your bare feet hanging out the window.

You Might Be a Redneck If . . .

Your favorite NASCAR souvenir is the result of a wreck.

There are more than six vehicles
under tarps in your yard.

☆

You've ever gotten carbon monoxide poisoning
while driving your own vehicle.

You Might Be a Redneck If . . .

You still own every tire you ever bought.

☆

The only time you buy shoe polish is to write
"For Sale" on your car.

☆

You've ever experienced road rage in your own driveway.

☆

Your pickup truck and wife are the same age.

☆

The most valuable part of your car is the gas in the tank.

☆

You can't find your gas and brake pedals
under fast-food wrappers.

You Might Be a Redneck If . . .

You've broken a speed limit in reverse.

Starting your car involves popping the hood.

☆

You can tell your car is low on oil by looking at the garage floor.

You Might Be a Redneck If . . .

You have a rag for a gas cap.

☆

Mechanics working on your car
don't know where to start.

☆

You've ever got into a fight over an inner tube.

☆

Opening your driver's-side window requires both hands.

☆

Your car has traveled more than three miles with you
steering and your wife pushing.

☆

You've ever siphoned gas from your lawn mower
to put in your truck.

You Might Be a Redneck If . . .

Your car gets rear-ended and you don't care.

☆

You think recycling means going home from work.

☆

You've waited in line to see a motorcycle jump 20 buses.

☆

Your hair salon is also an auto parts store.

☆

The crack in your windshield is longer than your arm—
and has been for more than a year.

☆

You've ever gone joyriding on a stolen bulldozer.

You were smoking in your driver's license photo.

Your husband spray-paints the upholstery
of your car to make it look new.

☆

The trunk of your car is tied down
and you're not hauling anything.

You Might Be a Redneck If . . .

Your RV is bigger than your house.

☆

Every vehicle you own has a winch.

☆

Your living room sofa came out of a Chevrolet.

☆

You've ever towed another car
using panty hose and duct tape.

☆

Your phone is mobile but your car isn't.

☆

You've ever given a stolen road sign
as a graduation present.

You Might Be a Redneck If...

You own more cars than socks.

☆

Your car used to be a police car.

☆

You work on your car when there's nothing wrong with it.

☆

You've waited in line overnight for a tire sale.

☆

The same cassette has been in your car stereo
for more than a decade.

☆

You've ever had your picture taken next to a Dale
Earnhardt Coke machine.

Home
Howm

Between kids and pets, our house looks like what's left over at the end of a garage sale. Our motto is, "If it ain't broke, it ain't ours."

My wife has this little statue. It used to be a ballerina, but now it just looks like the victim of a tragic farming accident. We have crayon murals on every wall—my oldest daughter claims the dog colored them. Our sofa doubled as a trampoline for years, so now if you sit in the wrong place, you can't have kids.

My youngest daughter has discovered the handle on the side of the toilet. She makes stuff disappear quicker than David Copperfield—combs, sunglasses, tubes of toothpaste. We're pretty sure she flushed the remote control because every time we go to the bathroom the TV comes on.

You Might Be a Redneck If . . .

A tree falls through your roof and you decide to leave it.

☆

Your answering machine message begins, "If you're calling about the free puppies . . ."

☆

You turn on your sprinkler and tell your kids it's a water park.

☆

The diploma hanging in your den includes the words "Trucking Institute."

☆

Your coffee table is also a cooler.

☆

Your best china traces the career of Loretta Lynn.

You Might Be a Redneck If . . .

Your satellite dish has more square footage than your home.

Any of your front room furniture is inflatable.

☆

You can't remember what the blue tarp in your front yard is covering.

You Might Be a Redneck If . . .

Your dog's so mean
you have to pick up your mail in town.

☆

Baby-sitters never work for you more than once.

☆

Your neighbor has ever asked to borrow a quart of beer.

☆

Your most expensive piece of art is held up
with thumbtacks.

☆

Directions to your house include
"turn off the paved road."

☆

Your kids trip over the Christmas lights
while hunting Easter eggs.

You Might Be a Redneck If . . .

Thanksgiving dinner was ruined because you ran out of ketchup.

You Might Be a Redneck If . . .

You always cancel the subscription and keep the free gift.

☆

The only cordless phone you have is the one your wife ripped out of the wall when she caught you talking to your girlfriend.

☆

You buy groceries, bait, and lottery tickets at the same place.

☆

You get a clear picture only when the cat sits on the TV.

☆

There are hoof prints on your carpet.

☆

You've been on TV more than once describing what the tornado sounded like.

You Might Be a Redneck If . . .

You've ever pawned a Beanie Baby.

The oil stain in your driveway
was once a barbecue sandwich.

☆

You have a Bud Light pool-table light
hanging over your dining room table.

You Might Be a Redneck If . . .

It takes you longer than two hours
to check all of your lottery tickets.

☆

You have separate mortgages on your home
and the land it's parked on.

☆

Your bathroom has a different mailing address
from your house.

☆

The hedge around your house is full of empty beer cans.

☆

You've ever had to shoot the lock off
your own front door.

☆

Your mailman wears a bee net and snake boots.

You Might Be a Redneck If . . .

Getting a package from the post office requires
a full tank of gas in the truck.

☆

Your yard has ever been the proposed site for a landfill.

☆

The neighbors refer to your doublewide on a sand mound
as "the mansion on the hill."

☆

Your gazebo is an old satellite dish held up by PVC pipes.

☆

You think orange peels left
on the coffee table are potpourri.

☆

You didn't put the pink plastic flamingos
in your front yard as a joke.

You Might Be a Redneck If . . .

FedEx stops at your house only for directions.

☆

The original color of your carpet is an unsolved mystery.

☆

You've ever driven around looking
for your porch roof after a bad storm.

☆

You spray-painted your dead shrubbery green.

☆

You call anyone who completes eighth grade "Brains."

☆

Your property has been mistaken for a recycling center.

You Might Be a Redneck If . . .

Your wife has a Jell-O mold
that looks like Elvis.

The garbage truck mistakenly takes your lawn furniture.

☆

You removed your bathroom door so you could watch TV
from the commode.

You Might Be a Redneck If . . .

You've ever hitchhiked to the liquor store.

☆

Your children's night-light is a neon beer sign.

☆

Hail hits your house and you have to take it
to the body shop for an estimate.

☆

Your dog passes gas and you claim it.

☆

You're saving up to "gravel" your driveway.

☆

The major decisions in your life were made
with the help of a Magic 8 Ball.

You Might Be a Redneck If . . .

The second thing you say after answering the phone is "Sitting around, drinking beer."

YEAH?

You Might Be a Redneck If . . .

You have a framed portrait of a hog.

Your Christmas ornaments are hung with paper clips.

☆

The phone number for a pizza delivery company is written on the wall above your phone.

You Might Be a Redneck If . . .

One of the blankets on your bed says
"Property of U-Haul."

☆

You open your walk-in beer cooler with a Clapper.

☆

Your mailing address includes the word "holler."

☆

You don't know a single joke clean enough
to tell the preacher.

☆

You've ever had Christmas dinner on a Ping-Pong table.

☆

Friends see your sunglasses lying on the counter and their
first thought is "Elvis is alive!"

You Might Be a Redneck If . . .

Your TV's remote control is your son Junior.

BACK IT UP TWO CLICKS...

You've been photographed with a prize-winning vegetable.

☆

The diving contest at the family reunion was ruined because your pool went flat.

You Might Be a Redneck If . . .

Property downwind of your home is virtually worthless.

☆

You've lived in three different homes at the same address.

☆

Someone knocks on your front door
and your back door rattles.

☆

You buy things you don't want
just because they're on sale.

☆

The bloodmobile will not visit your trailer park.

☆

You've ever heard "I told you it was loaded"
while staring at a hole in your ceiling.

You Might Be a Redneck If . . .

You have a hook in your shower to hang your hat on.

☆

You've ever videotaped a yard sale.

☆

There is a Jack Daniel's poster in your living room.

☆

You've ever tried to jump-start the battery in your watch.

☆

You are famous for your impression
of a dog choking on a chicken bone.

☆

The giant box of kitchen matches on the back of the
toilet was given to you by your children.

You Might Be a Redneck If . . .

You keep a can of Raid on your kitchen table.

☆

Your toilet paper has page numbers on it.

☆

The slipcover on your sofa used to be a shower curtain.

☆

People drive from miles away to look at your grandma's underpants hanging on the clothesline.

☆

You have to mow around a refrigerator and a bed frame.

☆

Your security system is the latch on your screen door.

You Might Be a Redneck If . . .

Your mailbox holds up one end of your clothesline.

The school principal has your number on speed dial.

☆

You have the entire WWF Slurpee cup collection proudly displayed on a shelf in your trailer.

You Might Be a Redneck If . . .

Strangers knock on your door mistakenly thinking you're having a yard sale.

Your air conditioner is louder than your TV.

☆

You flush the toilet and the dog thinks
you're giving him fresh water.

You Might Be a Redneck If...

All your kids' toys came free with a hamburger.

☆

Your previous two homes are rotting in the back pasture.

☆

You have ever tried to use food stamps to mail a watermelon.

☆

The man from the power company threatens to cut off your service, and you threaten to cut off something of his in return.

☆

You price everything really high at your yard sale in hopes that no one will buy it.

☆

You prominently display a gift you bought at Graceland.

You Might Be a Redneck If . . .

There's a grave in your yard.

Your tablecloth was delivered by the paperboy.

☆

The only thing your credit card is good for is scraping frost off your windshield.

You Might Be a Redneck If . . .

Your tools are worth more than your car.

☆

The only newspapers you read are sold in the checkout
line of the grocery store.

☆

You have Pabst Blue Ribbon on tap
anywhere in your house.

☆

You move your couch and find 14 cigarette lighters,
$1.37 in change, and a six-year-old *TV Guide.*

☆

You've been involved in a fistfight at a yard sale.

☆

The neighbors call 911 every time
you use the barbecue grill.

You Might Be a Redneck If . . .

There are eight chairs on your porch,
but none of them is safe to sit on.

☆

You need pliers to change the channel on your TV.

☆

You have a lava lamp over five feet tall.

☆

The most common phrase heard in your house is
"Somebody go jiggle the handle!"

☆

You take out a home improvement loan to buy a new
camper shell.

☆

Your aboveground pool is used for storage.

Making your bed involves moving at least three animals.

You Might Be a Redneck If . . .

You get new yard furniture every time the creek floods.

☆

The only private club you've ever belonged
to is Sam's Wholesale Club.

☆

There's a hole in the ozone layer
directly above your house.

☆

Your landscaping includes corn and squash.

☆

You view duct tape as a long-term investment.

☆

Your wife's jewelry box plays
"Beast of Burden" when opened.

You Might Be a Redneck If . . .

You are famous for your homemade squash wine.

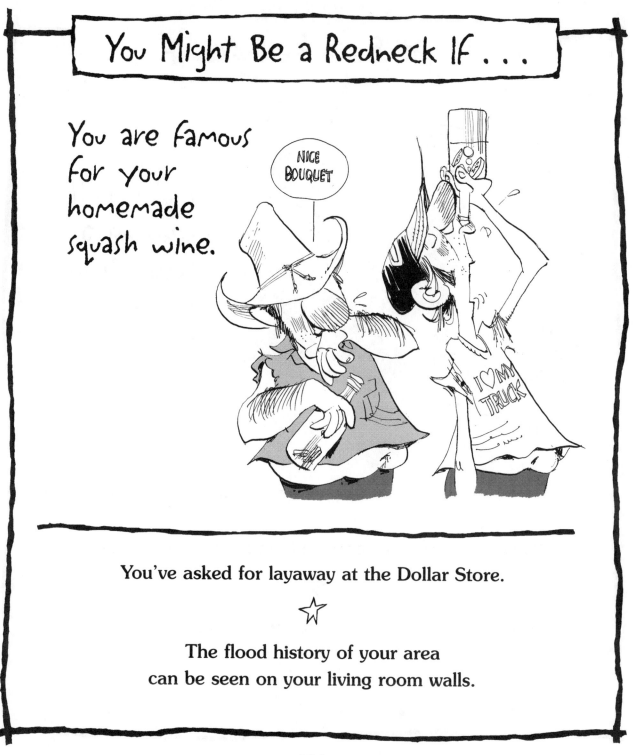

You've asked for layaway at the Dollar Store.

☆

The flood history of your area
can be seen on your living room walls.

You Might Be a Redneck If . . .

You're still keeping a goldfish in the plastic bag you won it in.

You can't spell your name without looking at your belt.

☆

The seats on your porch used to be seats in your car.

You Might Be a Redneck If . . .

You enjoy full cable TV service
when your neighbor leaves his curtains open.

☆

At least one corner of your bed is supported by a tire.

☆

There are orange road cones in your living room.

☆

You used Pam for shoe polish.

☆

The only pool you've ever owned is a cesspool.

☆

Neighbors call to say they've found your husband
in their yard.

Going to the bathroom in the middle of the night requires shoes and a flashlight.

There are more clothes on your floors
than in your drawers.

☆

You can name the entire cast of *The Dukes of Hazzard*
but not your congressmen.

You Might Be a Redneck If . . .

There's graffiti on the bathroom wall in your own house.

☆

You permanently have someone staying on your couch.

☆

Your wife's laundry basket used to be a grocery cart.

☆

The tallest building you've ever seen was a water tower.

☆

The box your TV came in has also served as a clubhouse, a laundry basket, and a playpen.

☆

Neighborhood kids knock on your door as a dare.

You Might Be a Redneck If . . .

You grow your own chewing tobacco.

☆

Realtors refuse to sell your home.

☆

Your front yard doubles as a go-cart track.

☆

There are fewer than six last names
in your local phone book.

☆

There's a belch on your answering machine greeting.

☆

Your garbage man is confused about
what goes and what stays.

You Might Be a Redneck If . . .

You have a tire swing in your house.

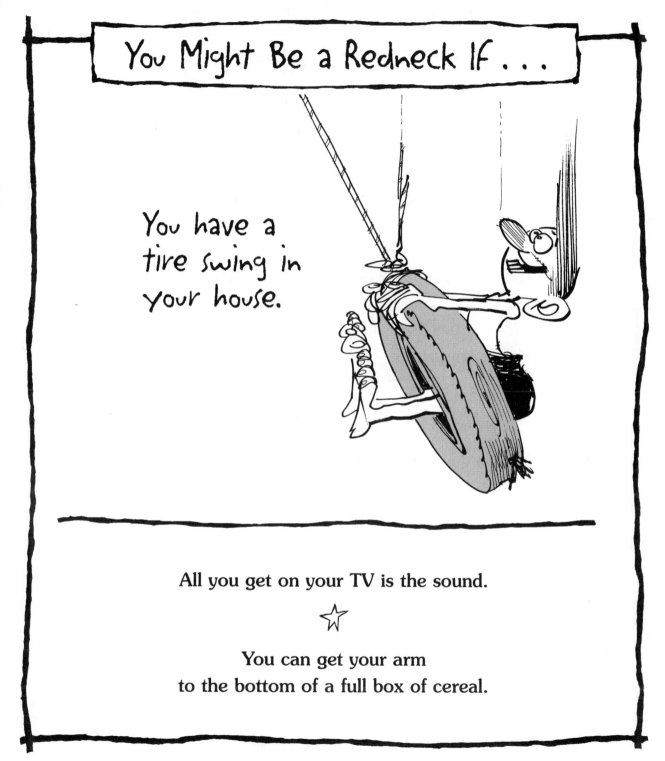

All you get on your TV is the sound.

☆

You can get your arm
to the bottom of a full box of cereal.

You Might Be a Redneck If . . .

Your living room curtains are beach towels.

☆

You clean your house with a water hose.

☆

The house feels a bit lonely when winter comes
and the last fly dies.

☆

You've ever peed your name in the snow.

☆

Anything in your home is running off a car battery.

☆

Your home has ever appeared on a humorous postcard.

You Might Be a Redneck If . . .

Your yard has more than 10 ceramic figurines.

You think "prime real estate"
is the chair next to the space heater.

☆

No matter which side of the track you live on,
it's the wrong side.

You Might Be a Redneck If . . .

You can pick objects up off the floor with your toes.

There is more carpet on your toilet than on your floors.

☆

The lawn-care service never leaves a flyer
on your front door.

You Might Be a Redneck If . . .

Your houseplants aren't in pots.

☆

There's a jukebox at your church.

☆

When you say, "Let's hit the hay," you actually mean it.

☆

There's no screen in your screen door.

☆

The shower runs cold when your neighbor
flushes his commode.

☆

Your wife got Caller ID so she'd know
which bar you're in.

You Might Be a Redneck If . . .

Your backyard smoker used to be a rest-stop trash can.

☆

You can't remember where your lawn mower is.

☆

There are more kids than groceries in your shopping cart.

☆

You answer all phone calls with "Check's in the mail."

☆

The dogcatcher calls for backup
when he goes to your house.

☆

You pay $1,200 a year to store $300 worth of stuff.

9 to 5
Nyne tu Fyve

When I turned 16, I went looking for a job. My dad had instilled a strong work ethic in me . . . and had also cut off my allowance.

Being quite intelligent, I knew I didn't want to do any work involving hot tar for $5 an hour. So I applied for a job at Six Flags over Georgia, assuming I'd get a fun job like operating the roller coaster. Instead, after my interview they said, "We've given your talents a lot of thought, and we've decided that you'll be sewing names on hats."

Sewing? Me? The job was as difficult as it was embarrassing, but I needed the money. I practiced for a month before the park opened, sewing the 100 most common names onto hats—John, Jane, David, Mary, Brent, Brittany, and so on.

Finally the park opened and I greeted my first customer. A small girl, accompanied by her smiling parents, picked out a sailor hat.

"Would you like me to sew your name on the hat?" I asked.

"Yes," she said politely.

"OK. And what is your name?"

"Cajavanetta," she answered.

CAJAVANETTA?

Somewhere (probably in therapy) there's a grown woman with a keepsake hat, embroidered with the name *CarlAnnette*, that her parents bought her when she was a child. That's as close as I could come.

You Might Be a Redneck If . . .

You've ever written your résumé on a cocktail napkin.

☆

You call your boss "dude."

☆

The biggest sign on your place
of business says "Minnows."

☆

You've held a business lunch at a vending machine.

☆

You made up your Social Security number.

☆

Your business mailing address is c/o Waffle House.

You're running a business from a pay phone.

You Might Be a Redneck If . . .

Every job you've had paid daily.

☆

You have a tattoo that says "Born to bag groceries."

☆

Your favorite topless bar
is the one where your daughters work.

☆

You list "beginner's luck" as a skill on a job application.

☆

Your work gloves double as Kleenex.

☆

You've ever been fired from a construction job
because of appearance.

You Might Be a Redneck If . . .

Your wife's job requires her to wear an orange vest.

You think the stock market has a fence around it.

You Might Be a Redneck If . . .

You don't need a clean shirt to go to work.

☆

You list "staring" among your hobbies.

☆

Your main business sign has three misspelled words.

☆

Three generations of your family are currently working at McDonald's.

☆

Your primary source of income is a pool stick.

☆

You advertise on the inside walls of portable toilets.

You've ever been paid in tomatoes.

You Might Be a Redneck If...

Your wife's work phone number begins with 1-900.

☆

You wake up early but still get to work late.

☆

You think "airing your dirty laundry"
means walking to work.

☆

You've skipped work for a sidewalk sale.

☆

You were ever fired for shooting spitballs.

☆

Your retirement plans include getting your own place.

You Might Be a Redneck If . . .

You think common stock
is a pig owned by more than one person.

☆

The family business requires a lookout.

☆

Your new job promotion means the company foots the
bill to have your name sewn on your shirts.

☆

Your wife regards removing her bra as a job skill.

☆

You've ever missed work because of chigger bites.

☆

You spend 40 hours a week at Wal-Mart
but don't work there.

The receptionist is responsible for checking the rattraps at your place of business.

You Might Be a Redneck If...

You were late to work because a cow
was lying in the middle of the road.

☆

You won't work on Garth's birthday.

☆

Your company went out of business
because your ladder broke.

☆

You ask to open a savings account and the teller asks,
"With what?"

☆

You've worn anything tie-dyed to a job interview.

☆

Your résumé includes your high scores on video games.

You Might Be a Redneck If . . .

You see a sign that says "Just say no to crack," and it reminds you to pull up your jeans.

Coworkers start a petition
over the contents of your lunches.

☆

You carry a case of beer to your tax audit.

You Might Be a Redneck If . . .

You sell rabbits out of your car.

☆

Your wife's work uniform has no top.

☆

The stock market crashes
and it doesn't affect you one bit.

☆

Your lifetime goal is to own your own fireworks stand.

☆

You wake up in the morning already dressed for work.

☆

Your financial planner told you to buy lottery tickets.

Partyin'
Par-tee-un

Single people don't think a party is successful unless the cops are called. It's the same scene every time they arrive: 100 drunks trying to act like they're not.

"Officer Jones, come on in," says the self-proclaimed spokesman who thinks he's sober. "Could I get you something to drink? Just a little joke, officer.

"I'm glad you came, 'cause I want to report a crime. Larry puked in the aquarium. Hey, while you're here, if I lie down on the sidewalk, will you draw my picture with that chalk y'all carry?"

Some people slept where they fell. You'd get up the next day thinking you were in Jonestown. You'd try to wake people you didn't even know. "Hey, man with no pants and fireman's helmet on, you have to go home now."

I once attended a toga party from which I walked home naked. It was only a couple of blocks, and it might have been raining. I can't remember. I'm still trying to figure out where I had my key. If you know, please don't tell me.

You Might Be a Redneck If . . .

You've ever paid for a six-pack of beer with pennies.

☆

You hired a stripper for your class reunion.

☆

Defending your sister's honor is a full-time job.

☆

You think cow tipping should be an Olympic sport.

☆

Your mother gives you tips on how to sneak liquor
into sports events.

☆

You've ever started a petition to have the national
anthem changed to "Freebird."

You Might Be a Redneck If . . .

You consider a six-pack of beer and a bug zapper quality entertainment.

Jack Daniel's makes your list of most admired people.

☆

You play strip poker at family reunions.

You Might Be a Redneck If . . .

You hope heaven is kind of like Hooters.

☆

You're receiving disability payments as the result
of a mechanical bull accident.

☆

You've used food stamps on a date.

☆

The most fun you've ever had involved water balloons
and a Ferris wheel.

☆

You've ever lit a cigarette with an arc welder.

☆

You need only one more hole punched in your card
before you get a freebie at the House of Tattoos.

You Might Be a Redneck If . . .

A man asks you to dance and you take off your clothes and climb on a table.

You Might Be a Redneck If . . .

Your last words before losing consciousness have ever been "Hey, y'all! Watch this!"

You Might Be a Redneck If . . .

You continue to show your cleavage years
after anyone wants to see it.

☆

In preparation for a romantic evening, you stop
by the grocery store for a bottle of Mr. Bubble.

☆

Your favorite "charity" is the one that dances
at the topless club.

☆

You've ever beaten someone up
because they had a library card.

☆

You've woken yourself up while breaking wind.

☆

You think French onion dip is an exotic tobacco product.

You Might Be a Redneck If . . .

The highlight of your parties is when you flip out your false teeth.

You Might Be a Redneck If . . .

A significant portion of your income
is spent on table dances.

☆

You've ever had to scratch your sister's name out of a
message that begins, "For a good time call . . ."

☆

There is a laminated picture of Rambo
on your headboard.

☆

You wake up at night shouting, "Bingo!"

☆

Your idea of a really big time
is shooting rats at the dump.

☆

You've ever wrestled your mama for the last can of beer.

You Might Be a Redneck If . . .

The nearest liquor store is brewing in your basement.

☆

You've ever attended a dance at the bus station.

☆

You pawned your grandfather's pocket watch because you needed beer money for the weekend.

☆

You ask for a senior citizen discount in a topless bar.

☆

You've ever bought a round of pickled pigs' feet.

☆

Your boob job paid for itself within six months.

You Might Be a Redneck If . . .

Your dog can smoke a cigarette.

You honk your horn during love scenes at the drive-in.

☆

You've ever hollered, "Rock the house, Bubba!"
during a piano recital.

You Might Be a Redneck If . . .

A man lights your cigarette and you show him your bra.

☆

You've ever head-butted a vending machine.

☆

You always start a story with the words, "Y'all ain't gonna believe this . . ."

☆

You refer to hot sex as "relative humidity."

☆

You've ever made love in a car . . . that was being towed.

☆

Your wife has been involved in more than six bar brawls in the last two weeks.

You Might Be a Redneck If . . .

You think *The Nutcracker* is something you did off the high dive.

You Might Be a Redneck If . . .

You've ever been too drunk to fish.

You were naked under your high school graduation robe.

☆

The local tattoo parlor runs specials
on your sister's name.

You Might Be a Redneck If . . .

You know more than 20 party tricks involving cigarettes.

☆

Three weeks after the circus, you're still talking about the elephant's accident.

☆

You've ever belched into a karaoke machine.

☆

You go to the Laundromat to pick up women.

☆

You've ever mixed drinks in an aquarium.

☆

You regularly answer the question, "What have you been doing lately?" with, "Partyin'."

You talk back to characters
on a movie screen.

You Might Be a Redneck If . . .

You've ever used a bar stool as a weapon.

☆

You know that your wheelbarrow
will hold ten 12-packs iced down.

☆

You consider dating second cousins as "playing the field."

☆

The local funeral parlor has a happy hour
before every burial.

☆

You've ever waved at traffic from your front porch
wearing nothing but your underwear.

☆

You think Chablis is the name
of last month's *Playboy* centerfold.

You Might Be a Redneck If . . .

You think "safe sex" is when the participants
are married to each other.

You've seen Elvis this week.

When people talk about the Big Easy,
you think they are referring to your ex-girlfriend.

You've ever taken reading material
into an airplane restroom.

You've ever stood in line to have your picture taken
with a freak of nature.

Your best pickup line for women is written
on your baseball cap.

You Might Be a Redneck If . . .

You've ever been the first person in
or the last person out of a video arcade.

☆

Your wife owns a camouflage nightie.

☆

You've ever left Santa Claus a PBR and a Slim Jim.

☆

Your Friday night consists
of lots of Budweiser and a mechanical bull.

☆

All the holes in your jeans came from buckshot
and barbed wire fences.

☆

You've ever slow danced in a Waffle House.

You've ever run down a bowling lane and slid into the pins.

You can burp the entire chorus of "Jingle Bells."

☆

Your dates regularly expect you to light their cigars.

You Might Be a Redneck If . . .

You've written a check for less than a dollar.

☆

Somebody hollers, "Hoe down!"
and your girlfriend hits the floor.

☆

You've ever used a video camera at a funeral.

☆

You openly wept when Pamela Lee
had her implants removed.

☆

You are famous in your neighborhood for your bonfires.

☆

You've never been conscious
at the end of the Super Bowl.

You Might Be a Redneck If . . .

You've ever asked a widow for her phone number at the funeral home.

Girls' night out is held at the Laundromat.

☆

You have taken an inner tube up a ski lift.

You Might Be a Redneck If . . .

You've been ejected from a bingo game.

☆

You refer to your van as "the Love Machine."

☆

The experience of your favorite restaurant
is enhanced by video tokens.

☆

You've ever used a bathtub as a punch bowl.

☆

The first drive-in movie you saw
was from across the road.

☆

When you refer to your "laptop," you're talking
about the dance you paid for last weekend.

You Might Be a Redneck If . . .

You've ever hypnotized a chicken.

☆

The morning after your last party,
you woke up in a bathtub.

☆

You know all the verses of the *Hee Haw* song.

☆

The most expensive meal you ever bought
came with a moist towelette.

☆

You've ever skinny-dipped in an inflatable pool.

☆

Your idea of an exciting time is throwing a piece of meat
out into the yard and watching the dogs fight over it.

Health & Hygiene
Helth n' Hi-jeen

I first chewed tobacco when I was in the ninth grade. Everybody else on the baseball team did it, so I figured I might as well. I quickly learned that you did *not* want to swallow your chew. Even a little juice will make you green with nausea and your buddies red with laughter.

Chewing was never a big hit with the women, so we usually didn't chew around them. I've never heard a woman say, "You know what I really like about Harvell? It's when he chews that tobacco and it makes his breath stinky and his teeth yellow. And we have little cups full of spit all over the house. That just really turns me on."

I gotta admit, any woman who chewed tobacco wasn't on our "must date" list. There's just something about a little brown drool in the corner of a woman's mouth that doesn't turn me on. But any day now I expect to see a *Playboy* spread on "Women Who Chew."

You Might Be a Redneck If . . .

You think an optimist is an eye doctor.

☆

You've discovered the limit of a restaurant's
"all you can eat" policy.

☆

You give up smoking
for three hours every New Year's Day.

☆

Most of the socks you own allow you to cut some
of your toenails while wearing them.

☆

You get Odor-Eaters as a Christmas present.

☆

Your midwife asks for an ashtray.

You Might Be a Redneck If . . .

You bring a bar of soap to the public pool.

You've ever cooked with WD-40.

☆

You go to the church Easter egg hunt
and carry a saltshaker in your shirt pocket.

You Might Be a Redneck If . . .

You think Tang is a member of the fruit group.

☆

The dentist in your town filed for bankruptcy.

☆

You've ever been to the emergency room
to have something removed from your nose.

☆

You've changed a diaper on a Denny's table.

☆

You punish your children
by taking away their chewing tobacco.

☆

You put beer on your cereal.

You Might Be a Redneck If . . .

Your kids have a three-day-old Kool-Aid mustache.

You think steroids are something you put Preparation H on.

☆

You haven't touched your toes in the last decade and neither has anybody else.

You Might Be a Redneck If . . .

You stare at a can of frozen orange juice
because it says "concentrate."

Everyone in the house learns something
from the potty training videotape.

You've ever barbecued Spam on the grill.

You have to take the entire day off work
to get your teeth cleaned.

You know for a fact that a sock
can be used as toilet paper.

Your toupee was made by your taxidermist.

You Might Be a Redneck If . . .

Birds are attracted to your beard.

You've been thrown out of the gym for staring.

☆

You have your appendix in a jar, sitting on your mantel, with the track lighting focused on it.

You Might Be a Redneck If . . .

You've ever been hospitalized after a chili cook-off.

☆

You put ketchup on Chinese food.

☆

Chiggers are included on your list
of top five hygiene concerns.

☆

You get your daily requirement of fiber from toothpicks.

☆

Your dentist dreads seeing you
more than you dread seeing him.

☆

You think PMS is a delivery service.

You Might Be a Redneck If . . .

You hold a frog and it worries about getting warts.

☆

You vacuum the sheets instead of washing them.

☆

Your toothbrush is a hand-me-down.

☆

The cleaners inform you
that they can't get the sweat stains out.

☆

You have used a potato peeler to remove a corn.

☆

You've ever given yourself a social disease.

You wet the bed and four other
people immediately know it.

Your wife uses auto touch-up paint on her nails.

☆

You have the cooking instructions
for macaroni and cheese memorized.

You Might Be a Redneck If . . .

You know more than 30 ways to prepare Spam.

☆

The Marlboro man is your idol.

☆

You have a drawer full of ketchup packets
and hot sauce from fast-food restaurants.

☆

You've ever relieved yourself in the neighbor's yard.

☆

You set your shoes outside and the flowers died.

☆

You think "the dishwasher is broke"
means your wife has no money.

The doctor who delivered your children also delivers your propane.

You Might Be a Redneck If . . .

You think toilet water is exactly that.

You've ever been scared to strike a match
in the bathroom.

☆

You spend most of your time
in the Laundromat so you can watch TV.

You Might Be a Redneck If . . .

You think Rolex is bathroom tissue.

☆

Sex education at your school included advice
on avoiding the steering wheel.

☆

Your wife makes you take Beano at bedtime.

☆

You made jewelry out of your gallstones.

☆

You're naked on laundry day.

☆

You've ever traded a nicotine patch for a long-neck beer.

You Might Be a Redneck If . . .

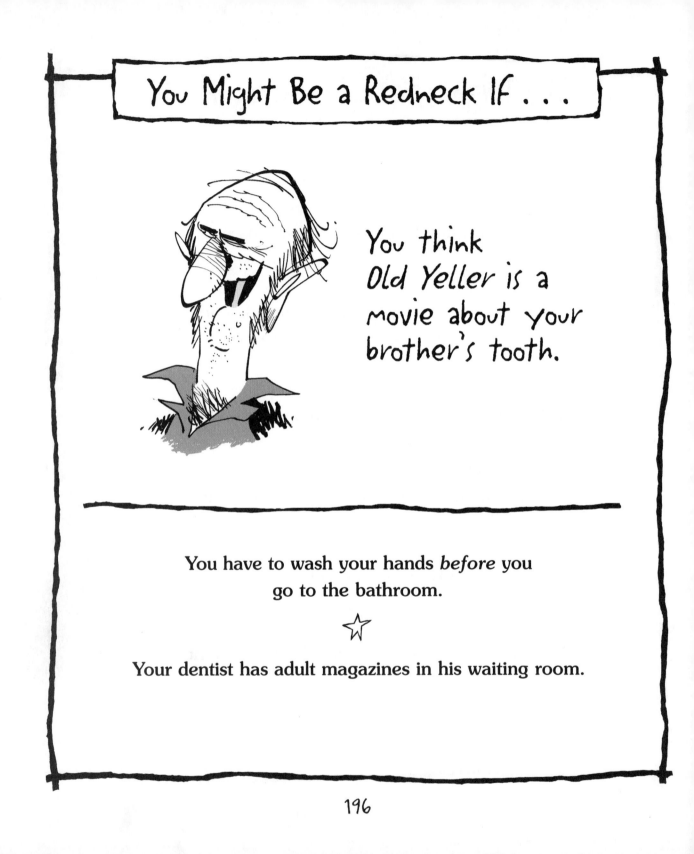

You think
Old Yeller is a
movie about your
brother's tooth.

You have to wash your hands *before* you
go to the bathroom.

☆

Your dentist has adult magazines in his waiting room.

You Might Be a Redneck If . . .

You strip naked to the waist to eat barbecue.

You think "social consciousness" refers
to how well you can hold your liquor.

You dye your hair and clean your floors
with the same stuff.

The only vegetable in your diet is the pickle
on a Big Mac.

You've ever purchased underwear
and worn it out of the store.

Your dentist has described you
as "the worst-case scenario."

You Might Be a Redneck If . . .

You have a prescription for antiperspirant.

☆

Nobody has ever asked your wife for one of her recipes.

☆

You don't think baseball players spit
and scratch too much.

☆

You've ever "hit on" somebody in a VD clinic.

☆

You pick your teeth from a catalog.

☆

You think beef jerky and Moon Pies
are two of the major food groups.

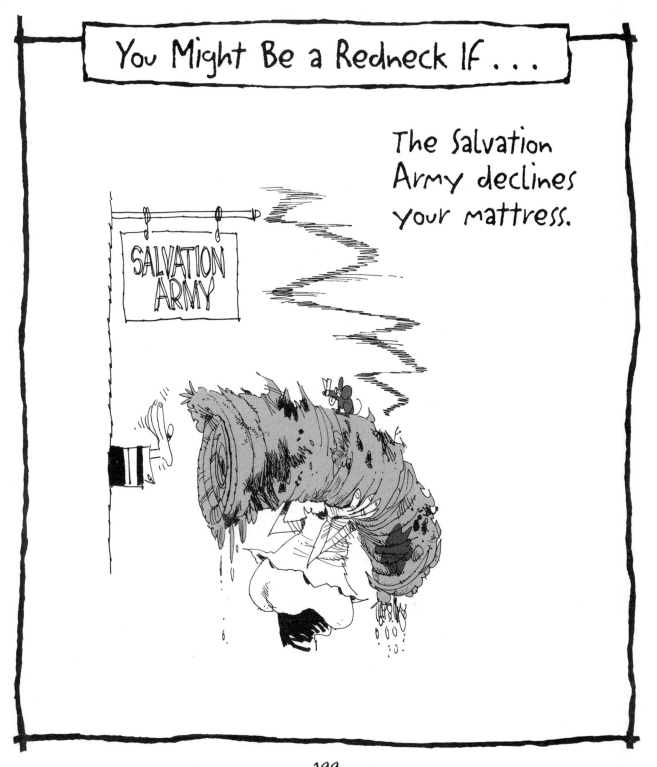

You Might Be a Redneck If . . .

Tying your shoelaces gives you a headache.

☆

You love lard sandwiches.

☆

You've earned more Marlboro miles than sky miles.

☆

You use the shaving cream made for tough beards . . .
and so does your husband.

☆

You wonder how service stations
keep their restrooms so clean.

☆

Your chili's secret ingredient comes from the bait shop.

You Might Be a Redneck If . . .

You can smoke a cigarette to the end without knocking off the ash.

You Might Be a Redneck If . . .

You think the "six to ten pounds" on the side of the Pampers box means how much the diaper will hold.

You're familiar with Copenhagen but have never heard of Denmark.

☆

You've ever had to shave your legs to get a pair of pants to fit.

You Might Be a Redneck If . . .

You've ever used panty hose as a coffee filter.

☆

You cut your toenails in front of company.

☆

Your cap violates a health code.

☆

You refer to McDonald's as the "Big M Supper Club."

☆

People can tell what you had for breakfast
by looking at your beard.

☆

You think NSYNC is where your dirty dishes are.

You Might Be a Redneck If . . .

You use a piece of bread as a napkin.

☆

Your doctor prescribes moonshine as a painkiller.

☆

Red Man Chewing Tobacco sends you a Christmas card.

☆

You clean your fingernails with a stick.

☆

Your exercise bike is currently on blocks.

☆

You think "hiding your valuables" means
putting the Nutter Butter cookies under the couch.

You Might Be a Redneck If . . .

You use a screwdriver to open your chewing tobacco.

☆

Your favorite suntan lotion is Crisco.

☆

You think Campho-Phenique is a miracle drug.

☆

Your kid's favorite teething ring
is the garden hose in the front yard.

☆

"Pass the buck" means you want seconds.

☆

You can drink beer through your nose.

You Might Be a Redneck If . . .

You've unstopped a sink with a shotgun.

You Might Be a Redneck If . . .

Your sneeze can disrupt TV reception.

☆

You spray Cheez Whiz directly into your mouth.

☆

You stockpile pork and beans.

☆

You think "eating right" means using a knife and fork.

☆

It's impossible to see food stains
on the fabric of your work uniform.

☆

You've ever fixed your false teeth with a glue gun.

You Might Be a Redneck If . . .

You've ever lost
a tooth opening
a beer bottle.

You think truffles are a brand of potato chips.

☆

You offer to give somebody the shirt off your back
and they don't want it.

You Might Be a Redneck If . . .

GOOD DOG!

You think a lavatory is a breed of dog.

You've ever been accused of lying through your tooth.

☆

Your pocketknife doubles as a toenail clipper and a cheese slicer.

You Might Be a Redneck If . . .

You can eat a McDonald's cheeseburger in one bite.

☆

You've ever plucked a nose hair with a pair of pliers.

☆

You think the four seasons
are onion, pepper, salt, and garlic.

☆

Your favorite recipe includes Vienna Sausage.

☆

Your masseuse uses lard.

☆

In your church's Christmas play,
two of the wise men smoked during the performance.

You Might Be a Redneck If . . .

Your favorite seafood is hush puppies.

☆

All of your dental visits are emergencies.

☆

You think the three most important things in life
are air, water, and mayonnaise.

☆

You carry Ziploc bags in your purse for leftovers.

☆

You've ever had a corn dog for breakfast.

☆

Your third-grade class had a no-smoking section.

You Might Be a Redneck If . . .

You've ever snuck a spit cup into church.

☆

You wash your car more often than your kids.

☆

Breakfast every morning is interrupted
by someone asking, "Anybody seen my teeth?"

☆

You've ever removed a wart with a firearm.

☆

People are scared to touch your bathrobe.

☆

Your wife serves Cheetos as a vegetable.

You Might Be a Redneck If . . .

You get an estimate from the barber before he cuts your hair.

You think Thunderbird is an acceptable wine choice with a bean burrito.

☆

Your two-year-old has more teeth than you do.

You Might Be a Redneck If . . .

You've ever used a cheese ball as a weapon.

☆

The Roto-Rooter man comes to your house and asks,
"What's that smell?"

☆

You have a recipe for catfish lasagna.

☆

Your medical plan is to not get sick.

☆

You forego a haircut
because there's not a clean bowl in the house.

☆

You think "going the extra mile" means using toothpaste.

You Might Be a Redneck If . . .

You've ever been to an ear, nose, and throat specialist to have a finger removed.

You Might Be a Redneck If . . .

You get your oil changed by your barber.

☆

You think a reservoir tip
is something they give you on fishing shows.

☆

You've ever picked your teeth with a menu.

☆

The Orkin man tells you, "Give up! You've lost."

☆

You've tightened a loose screw with your fingernail.

☆

Your idea of conservation is moving your Saturday night
bath to every other Saturday night.

You Might Be a Redneck If . . .

You make your own beef jerky.

☆

You'd taken three pregnancy tests
before you ever took a driving test.

☆

You own all the components of soap-on-a-rope
except the soap.

☆

You've ever used duct tape to repair dental work.

☆

You think potted meat on a saltine is an hors d'oeuvre.

☆

You didn't know you were cross-eyed
until you joined the army.

You Might Be a Redneck If . . .

You clean your hands daily with gasoline.

☆

Your dentist wanted to exhibit
your eyeteeth at a convention.

☆

There is more oil in your baseball cap than in your car.

☆

Your junior high grades suffered
because of morning sickness.

☆

You're using a Twister mat as a shower curtain.

☆

You think a "health kick" is smoking light cigarettes
and drinking wine coolers.

Fashion

Fa-shun

When you're dating, you can wear hip waders to a family dinner and your girlfriend thinks it's cute. But once you're married, the same outfit will evoke a familiar response: "You're not wearing *that*, are you?"

That is any clothing you owned before you got married. You'll wake up one day and find bags full of your favorite clothes marked "Charity," waiting on the front porch to be picked up.

I once came home from a trip and discovered that my wife had done me "a favor" by "cleaning out" my closet. I ripped open one of the bags on the front porch and said, "You can't get rid of this shirt! It's one of my favorites."

"But it's out of style," she said.

"Out of style? Are you kidding? I saw John Belushi wearing one just like it last night on TV."

"That's right," she said, "and he's been dead 15 years!"

I knew that, but I was waiting for it to come back into style.

You Might Be a Redneck If . . .

You've ever worn an "I'm with stupid" T-shirt
when you were out alone.

☆

Your most expensive shoes have numbers on the heels.

☆

You sew the legs back on your jeans
at the end of each summer.

☆

There is a six-inch gap between the bottom of your shirt
and the top of your pants.

☆

You've ever bought a used cap.

☆

You wore a tank top to your mother's funeral.

You Might Be a Redneck If . . .

Someone asks to see your ID and you show them your belt buckle.

You consider your softball uniform "dressy-casual."

☆

Your wife wears chip clips in her hair.

You Might Be a Redneck If . . .

You think a turtleneck is a key ingredient to soup.

☆

Your prom dress was knitted.

☆

All your favorite shirts came
with a two-pack purchase of cigarettes.

☆

You own a pair of homemade lizard-skin boots.

☆

Your panty line can be seen from 100 yards away.

☆

You actually wear shoes your dog brought home.

You Might Be a Redneck If . . .

Your wife's hairdo has ever been ruined by a ceiling fan.

You have a pair of cutoffs made from double knit pants.

☆

You think the three greatest inventions of all time are hot pants, four-wheelers, and ketchup.

You Might Be a Redneck If . . .

You bought your best pair of shoes
off the impulse rack by the cash register.

☆

Your belt buckle is bigger than your head.

☆

You know how to identify genuine cubic zirconia.

☆

Everybody you meet can tell
what kind of underwear you're wearing.

☆

You use bungee cords as suspenders.

☆

Your wife has to ask, "What color shoes do I have on?"

Your spring wardrobe mostly involves using scissors.

You Might Be a Redneck If . . .

You own a denim leisure suit.

☆

Your bridesmaids' dresses were based on XFL
cheerleader outfits.

☆

You've ever stolen clothes from a scarecrow.

☆

You were wearing a John Deere hat
in your senior picture.

☆

The only time you were ever in the dry cleaners
was to get out of the rain.

☆

You have to dress up the kids to go to Kmart.

You Might Be a Redneck If . . .

Your favorite cap says "Babymaker."

☆

You and your wife wear matching outfits to church.

☆

You grow your sideburns longer and fuller
because it looks so good on your sister.

☆

You buy brown sheets so you don't have to wash them.

☆

Every pair of shorts you own used to be pants.

☆

Your best shirt came from a rock concert.

You Might Be a Redneck If . . .

You've ever worn curlers and a bathrobe to a PTA meeting.

You know of at least six different ways to bend the bill of a baseball cap.

☆

You've ever worn cowboy boots with Bermuda shorts.

You Might Be a Redneck If . . .

Your wife's fur coat is shedding.

☆

Your wedding shirt had cutoff sleeves.

☆

You regularly answer the door in your underwear,
carrying a baseball bat.

☆

Everyone knows what color bra you're wearing.

☆

Your most expensive jacket is camouflage.

☆

You've worn your Waffle House uniform on a date.

You have to curl the sides of your cowboy hat so your wife can ride in the truck too.

You Might Be a Redneck If . . .

You attend a parent-teacher conference wearing flip-flops.

☆

Your mother's bra was featured on *That's Incredible.*

☆

You use Wite-Out to do a French manicure.

☆

You wore a three-day growth of beard
before Don Johnson did.

☆

You own a pair of knee-high moccasins.

☆

Your watchband is wider than any book you've ever read.

You Might Be a Redneck If . . .

You've ever bought lingerie at a yard sale.

You open beer bottles with your belt buckle.

☆

You wear overalls to save on the cost
of shirts and underwear.

You Might Be a Redneck If . . .

Your wear your Marlboro windbreaker to church.

☆

You've ever used a tablespoon as a shoehorn.

☆

The "No shirt, no shoes . . ."
rule deeply affected your family.

☆

Your best shoes used to be someone else's.

☆

You've ever worn suit pants without a shirt.

☆

Your grandmother wears a tank top without a bra.

You Might Be a Redneck If . . .

Your stomach is bigger than any shirt you own.

☆

You wear knee-high stockings with a skirt.

☆

Your shoelaces used to be baling wire.

☆

The collar on your dog
cost more than what you're wearing.

☆

You've ever been on television not wearing a shirt.

☆

Your first bra was a Wonderbra.

You Might Be a Redneck If . . .

You've ever worn shorts to a funeral home.

Your best jacket has an advertisement on the back.

☆

You've ever applied for a job while wearing a stocking cap.

You Might Be a Redneck If . . .

You've never owned an iron.

☆

You wear cowboy boots without socks.

☆

You prefer to walk the excess length
off your jeans rather than hem them.

☆

You wear a baseball cap to bed.

☆

Your waist measurement exceeds your bust measurement.

☆

Your wedding dress was leather.

You Might Be a Redneck If . . .

Strangers mistakenly think your children are already dressed for trick or treat.

You Might Be a Redneck If . . .

You tuck your shirt into your underpants.

☆

You think virgin wool comes from ugly sheep.

☆

Your name is in the *Guinness Book of World Records*
in the "sideburns" section.

☆

Your sexiest gown came from a hospital.

☆

Both you and your wife wore ponytails
on your wedding day.

☆

You broke a toe when you dropped your belt buckle on it.

The Law
Da Laaaw

Once a friend and I had been partyin' too hard too long, and being young and dumb at the time, I decided to drive us home. Somehow I confused the highway sign for I-85 with the speed limit, and before long there was a flashing red light in my rearview mirror.

"Good evening, officer. What seems to be the problem?" I asked.

He yanked the car door open and said, "The problem is that you're going to jail."

He was exactly right. After frisking me and confiscating my three-inch-long pocketknife, he escorted me to the county drunk tank.

Now, I'm not a vain person, but I was definitely the cutest drunk in the tank that night, and I was very worried about being asked to dance. Four long hours later, I was moved to the regular jail, where I spent another 24 hours before my friend's father-in-law bailed me out.

The DWI charge was eventually dropped, I eventually grew up and never drove under the influence again, and I eventually got my pocketknife back. When I went to reclaim it, a woman officer produced a box full of machetes, switchblades, daggers, and automatic weapons. She matched my claim check to the little pocketknife, looked up at me and said, "You got to be kidding." For once, I wasn't.

You Might Be a Redneck If . . .

Your dog was neutered by court order.

☆

More than one person at your class reunion
was on a weekend pass.

☆

You have a family portrait drawn by a courtroom artist.

☆

The only time you moved
was under a witness protection program.

☆

Your bass boat has been involved in a police chase.

☆

You've appeared on TV with your face digitally blurred.

Your high school annual is now a mug shot book for the police department.

You consider your license plate "personalized" because your father made it.

☆

All your home electronics have the serial numbers filed off.

You Might Be a Redneck If . . .

A judge sentences you to "the usual."

☆

You've ever been arrested
on an obscene mud-flap charge.

☆

Someone calls security every time you visit the mall.

☆

You are the legal heir to a fireworks stand.

☆

You've ever held up someone with a caulk gun.

☆

The FBI has more pictures of your family than you do.

You Might Be a Redneck If . . .

Your pocketknife has ever been referred to as "Exhibit A."

EXHIBIT A

You buy a police scanner to keep up with your relatives.

☆

The neighbor's rabbit disappears and the police question you first.

You Might Be a Redneck If . . .

A night on the town includes the city jail.

☆

The only words you say in court are "I dunno."

☆

Your biggest business worry is law enforcement.

☆

Your dad's cell number
has nothing to do with a telephone.

☆

You've ever taken out a restraining order
against your mother-in-law.

☆

The last time you test-drove a car,
it ended in a police chase.

You've ever been arrested for relieving yourself in an ice machine.

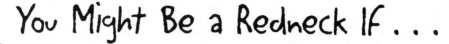

You Might Be a Redneck If . . .

Stealing road signs is a family outing.

☆

You moved to another state so you can buy beer
on Sundays.

☆

You've ever introduced someone as
"my court-appointed lawyer."

☆

The only diploma on your wall is from DUI school.

☆

You're driving the car being described
on the police scanner.

☆

Your three-year-old is trained to bring a beer
to any cops who show up at the door.

You Might Be a Redneck If . . .

You hear a siren and your first instinct is to hide.

☆

Your wife's brass knuckles
set off the airport security alarm.

☆

Local cops know you by your nickname.

☆

Your attorney begs you not to take the stand.

☆

The city council ever discussed your front yard.

☆

You can't schedule a family reunion
until after the parole board meets.

You Might Be a Redneck If . . .

STIFFSOCK COUNTY SHERIFF DEPT.
OA 649-442-9884
JULY 3, 1989

STIFFSOCK COUNTY SHERIFF DEPT.
OA 649-442-9884
JULY 3, 1989

The last photos of your mama were taken from the front and the side.

You get homesick watching *Cops* on TV.

☆

You're convinced that police can't see you because your truck is painted camouflage.

You Might Be a Redneck If . . .

You frisk everyone at your family reunions.

☆

Police ever drove you to the city limits.

☆

Your last keg party included a couple of 911 calls.

☆

The health inspector has threatened to close
your favorite restaurant three times in the past year.

☆

You got a speeding ticket while towing another vehicle.

☆

Your class voted you "Most likely to return fire."

You've ever been arrested for loitering.

☆

You have more previous convictions
than you have previous employers.

Your mother does not remove the Marlboro from her lips before telling the state patrolman to kiss her ass.

You joined a record club under a fake name.

☆

You've been up for parole more times than you've been up for promotion.

You Might Be a Redneck If . . .

You inherited a stolen road sign.

☆

Your parrot can say, "Open up, it's the police!"

☆

Tear gas was ever fired into your trailer.

☆

You think "taking the law into your own hands"
means giving the sheriff a hug.

☆

The best photo of you has a height chart as a backdrop.

☆

You're not allowed to mention
the game warden's name in the house.

You Might Be a Redneck If . . .

There is a lawsuit pending against your dog.

You've ever left a bingo game in handcuffs.

☆

Your neighbors think you're a detective because a cop always brings you home.

You Might Be a Redneck If . . .

You've practiced saying the words "not guilty."

☆

Police ever raided your storage unit.

☆

The last time you saw your daddy outside,
he was picking up trash . . . chained to three other guys.

☆

You disguise your voice when answering the phone.

☆

You can name more state penitentiaries
than state capitals.

☆

Your mother has ever been arrested for poaching.

You Might Be a Redneck If . . .

You ask the judge for a light.

☆

You've ever worn a wire to a family reunion.

☆

Your previous three cars were auctioned off by the police.

☆

You secretly get your firewood from your neighbor's yard.

☆

The crack in your toilet seat is named in a lawsuit.

☆

Police ever talked you down from a water tower.

You Might Be a Redneck If . . .

You've had more court dates than dinner dates.

☆

The neighbors started a petition
over your Christmas lights.

☆

You've ever committed a crime with a lawn mower.

☆

The local police go on alert
during your Super Bowl party.

☆

The last time off you had was for good behavior.

☆

Your monthly budget includes bail.

You Might Be a Redneck If . . .

The key to your city is a handcuff key.

☆

Your outdoor light used to be in a mall parking lot.

☆

The police come to talk to you
about your "tomato" plants.

☆

You've ever thrown up in a squad car.

☆

Your honeymoon was featured
on *Real Stories of the Highway Patrol*.

☆

The judge tells you shooting crows
is not a community service.

You Might Be a Redneck If . . .

You've turned in a family member for the reward.

☆

The only work your father ever did was supervised
by a man holding a shotgun.

☆

You've hot-wired a riding mower.

☆

You have Mason jars filled with stuff
the FBI can't identify.

☆

When the judge asked how you plead,
you said, "Whatever."

☆

You and your truant officer
shoot pool during school hours.

The Great Outdoors
Da Grate Owt-dorz

No woman, not even my mother or my wife, understands the pure pleasure of rising before daybreak in subfreezing temperatures and going out to sit in a tree for four or five hours, waiting for a deer to walk past. I have spent an entire vacation doing that and enjoyed every minute of it.

The spot in the tree—called a *stand*, even though you only sit in it—is an essential part of deer hunting. Surrounded by limbs, you are naturally camouflaged. Also, sitting up high reduces the chance that some other hunter will mistake your Day-Glo orange parka and bright red hat for a deer and shoot you. And finally, deer don't often look up. Even they can't understand why any man would spend his vacation sitting in a tree.

You Might Be a Redneck If . . .

You and your wife stay married for the sake of the dogs.

☆

Your taxidermist also does your taxes.

☆

People don't recognize your car
without a dead animal on the hood.

☆

Your grandmother reloads her own shotgun shells.

☆

You quit your job because deer season's fixin' to start.

☆

You've ever shot a beer can
while someone else was drinking out of it.

You Might Be a Redneck If . . .

You take your dog for a walk and you both use the tree at the corner.

You Might Be a Redneck If . . .

Your hobbies require dogs and a lantern.

☆

You've ever caught bugs
just so you could throw them in the bug-zapper.

☆

You know how to milk a goat.

☆

Your kid's birthday party activities
included a rabbit-skinning contest.

☆

You've ever cleaned fish in your living room.

☆

You and your dog are on the same medication.

You Might Be a Redneck If . . .

There is a stuffed possum mounted anywhere in your home.

Your doghouse and your living room
have the same shag carpet.

☆

You empty your pockets and there's just a pile of change,
bullets, and lint.

You Might Be a Redneck If . . .

Your wife has a set of earrings that you use as fishing lures.

You consider *Outdoor Life* deep reading.

☆

Putting your dog to sleep
involves a bowl of warm milk and a bedtime story.

You Might Be a Redneck If . . .

You are allowed to bring your dog to work.

☆

You've ever used a fishing boat to haul lumber.

☆

You can buy live bait and cold beer at your barbershop.

☆

In high school you were voted
"Most likely to fish from a bridge."

☆

Your kids hide the Easter eggs under cow patties.

☆

You've turkey hunted from a school bus.

You Might Be a Redneck If . . .

You celebrate your bird dog's birthday.

Thanks to your welding buddy and the plumbing supply store, you have a triple-barrel shotgun.

☆

You've ever gotten naked to retrieve a golf ball.

You Might Be a Redneck If . . .

You do your bird-watching through a rifle scope.

☆

Your landscape gardening features cattle skulls.

☆

The cat paw prints on your windshield are on the inside.

☆

You enjoy playing with bait more than you like to fish.

☆

You've ever celebrated your wife's birthday in a tree.

☆

You have no hubcaps on your car
because you're using them to feed your hunting dogs.

You Might Be a Redneck If . . .

Your first pet was a chicken.

☆

You know more than one way to catch an armadillo.

☆

The curtains in your living room are camouflage.

☆

You can play "The Star-Spangled Banner"
on your turkey call.

☆

Your fishing license is more precious to you
than your marriage license.

☆

You list dogs as dependents on your tax form.

When packing for vacation, your biggest decision is whether to use paper or plastic.

You Might Be a Redneck If . . .

You can entertain yourself for more than an hour with a flyswatter.

Your Christmas tree has a deer stand in it.

☆

You have 16 cats living in your yard
but can't get close enough to pet any of them.

You Might Be a Redneck If . . .

Your dog is the father of every dog in the neighborhood.

☆

The deer head over your fireplace
is wearing your Mardi Gras beads.

☆

You wouldn't even consider going to work without a gun.

☆

Your basketball hoop is a fishing net.

☆

You let your dog baby-sit your kids.

☆

You've ever hunted quail in the interstate median.

You Might Be a Redneck If . . .

You made a homemade hot tub with a trolling motor.

Your dog stops barking and you bury it.

☆

The only big bucks you've ever come into
are hanging over your fireplace.

You Might Be a Redneck If . . .

The dog can't watch you eat without gagging.

☆

You've ever shot at a "No Hunting" sign.

☆

You frequently quote
from *Turkey Strategies for Success*.

☆

You get poison ivy, chigger bites,
and fleas just walking to your mailbox.

☆

Your wife left you for last year's winner
of the hog-calling contest.

☆

Your car alarm eats dog food.

You Might Be a Redneck If...

You sent out birth announcements for your new puppies.

☆

Your Thanksgiving dinner was alive that morning.

☆

You sharpen knives for a lot of people, but it is not your occupation.

☆

The other guys in your hunting club chip in to buy you new long johns.

☆

You used a cheat sheet during your hunter's safety test.

☆

You've ever snuck a dog into the hospital for a visit.

You Might Be a Redneck If . . .

Your Thanksgiving centerpiece has ever been prepared by a taxidermist.

Your children catch frogs and lizards . . .
inside the house.

☆

The photo on your driver's license includes your dog.

You Might Be a Redneck If . . .

You list tick removal as a skill on your résumé.

☆

You've ever cracked crab legs with your shoe.

☆

Your lawn fertilizer was in your cow
about five minutes earlier.

☆

You often find stray animals in your living room.

☆

The plastic deer in your yard are not decorations—
they're practice targets.

☆

You've used a Styrofoam cooler in a pet's funeral.

You Might Be a Redneck If . . .

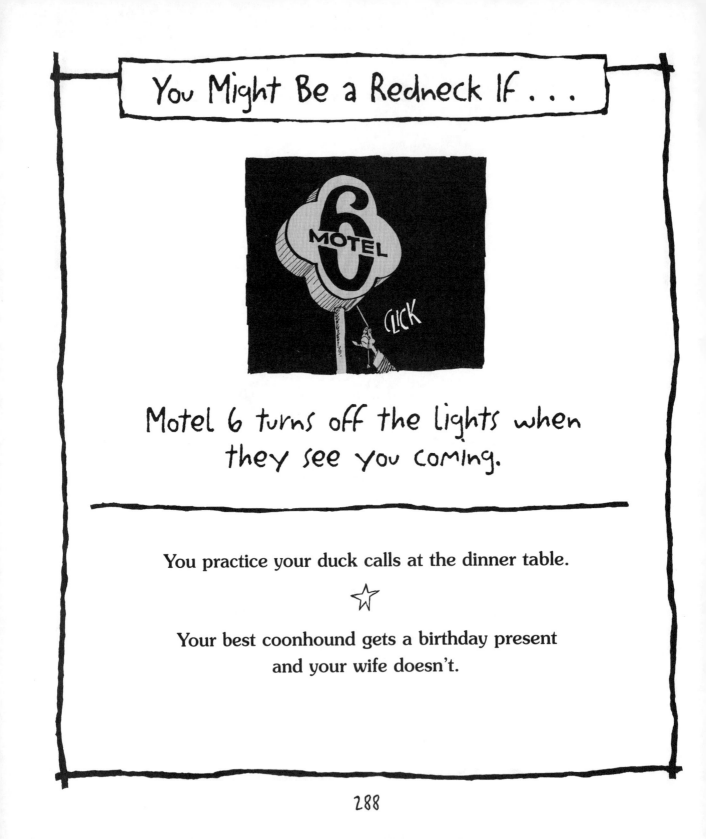

Motel 6 turns off the lights when they see you coming.

You practice your duck calls at the dinner table.

☆

Your best coonhound gets a birthday present and your wife doesn't.

You Might Be a Redneck If . . .

You practice casting in your yard.

You execute holds on your dog
while watching TV wrestling.

The recoil pad on your shotgun used
to be the cup of your wife's bra.

Your favorite hunting story includes,
"So I rolled down the window real quiet-like . . ."

You've ever used firecrackers to blow up an anthill.

Your brother had to cosign to get your deer mounted.

You Might Be a Redneck If . . .

You've given mouth-to-mouth resuscitation to a dog.

OH, DEATH... WHERE IS THY STING?

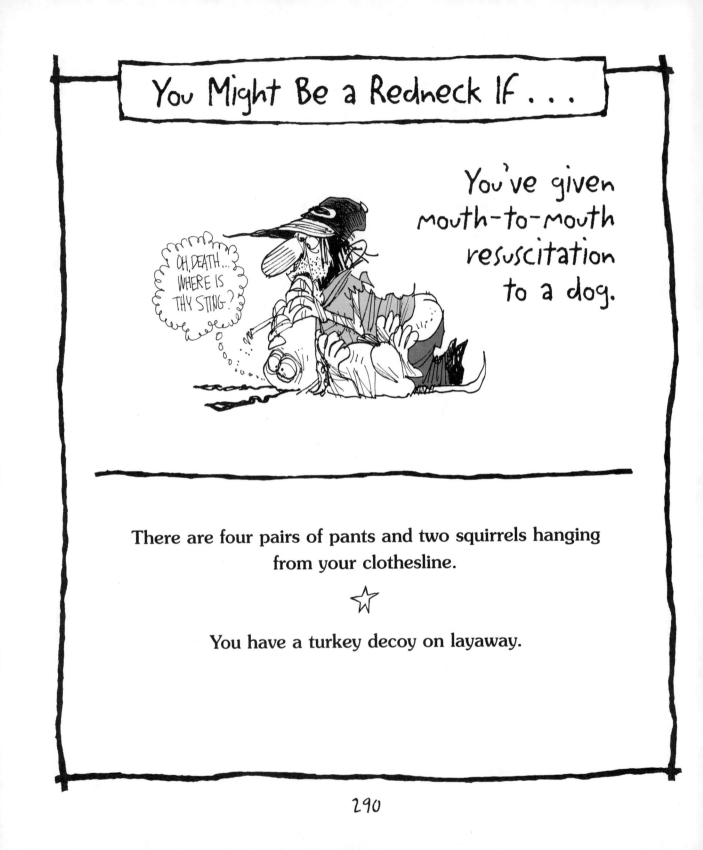

There are four pairs of pants and two squirrels hanging from your clothesline.

☆

You have a turkey decoy on layaway.

You Might Be a Redneck If . . .

Your deer lease costs more than your house.

☆

You've ever picked birdshot out of your fried chicken.

☆

You've ever sunk a rental paddleboat.

☆

Your wife can climb a tree faster than your cat.

☆

Your deceased hunting dog's tombstone
is bigger than your grandfather's.

☆

You think fast food is hitting a deer at 65 miles per hour.

You Might Be a Redneck If . . .

There is a restraining order on your pets.

☆

You consider turkey calling a second language.

☆

Your local newspaper has a front-page feature called
"Cow of the Week."

☆

You decorate your dog for Christmas.

☆

You've ever taken a deer skin to the dry cleaners.

☆

Your dog has a litter of puppies
on the living room floor and nobody notices.

You Might Be a Redneck If . . .

You've ever vacationed in a rest area.

You were kicked out of your dog's obedience school.

☆

Your house catches on fire and you run back
in to save the deer heads.

You Might Be a Redneck If . . .

Your doorbell is a dog.

☆

You go fishing with a generator and copper wire.

☆

You've bet on gator wrestling.

☆

Your kids can't use the sandbox because the cats do.

☆

You've ever hunted within 20 yards
of your child's swing set.

☆

You think a stock tip is advice on wormin' your hogs.

You Might Be a Redneck If . . .

Your mama tore her best dress
coon hunting.

You Might Be a Redneck If . . .

Your front porch collapses and kills more than three dogs.

You've ever shot dead limbs out of trees in your front yard.

☆

You've been to the emergency room more than three times to have a fishhook removed.

You Might Be a Redneck If . . .

You own a photo of your dog wearing dark glasses.

☆

There's an endangered species in your freezer.

☆

Your dogs always get to your trash before the garbage truck does.

☆

You've ever worn camouflage pants to church.

☆

You've followed the knife and gun show to more than one town.

☆

Your standard of living improves when you go camping.

You Might Be a Redneck If . . .

You keep catfish in your aquarium.

You Might Be a Redneck If . . .

Your kids can demonstrate how to rig a possum trap.

☆

You have no idea how many pets you have.

☆

You talk to your dog more than your wife.

☆

You've ever used a Weed Eater indoors.

☆

You videotape fishing shows.

☆

Callers can hear dogs barking
on your answering machine greeting.

You Might Be a Redneck If . . .

Your dogs sleep on your bed
and your wife sleeps on the sofa.

☆

You've ever taught cuss words to a parrot.

☆

Your butcher is also your taxidermist.

☆

You fly-fish with real flies.

☆

You've ever sucked snake venom from a dog.

☆

Santa Claus stopped coming
to see you after you shot at his reindeer.

You Might Be a Redneck If . . .

Your dog and your wallet are both on a chain.

You practice shooting your bow at work.

☆

Your pet bunny Fluffy was the hit of Easter morning
and then was served with sweet potatoes
at the Fourth of July picnic.

You Might Be a Redneck If . . .

You refer to your dog as "my youngest."

☆

You regard deer processing as an art form.

☆

Any of your children were conceived in a bass boat.

☆

You've driven more than 100 miles to look at a hog.

☆

You've ever been asked for your autograph
at a rattlesnake roundup.

☆

Your kids take rabbit sandwiches
to school in their lunch boxes.

You Might Be a Redneck If . . .

Your mounted deer head sports a baseball cap and sunglasses.

You Might Be a Redneck If . . .

Your most effective fishing lure is TNT.

☆

You've ever used hairspray to kill flying bugs.

☆

There are more than 10 cats living under your trailer.

☆

Your dog buries bones in the middle of your living room.

☆

You have to honk your horn when pulling into your
driveway to keep from killing chickens.

☆

Your deer stand has an address.

Your checks feature pictures of dogs fighting.

You would rather fish than have sex.

☆

You've hit a deer with your car . . . deliberately.

You Might Be a Redneck If . . .

Your dog has his own recliner.

☆

Your lawn mowers are named Nanny and Billy.

☆

There's ammunition in your Christmas stocking.

☆

Your chicken house used to be a school bus.

☆

Dogs chase your truck every morning
when you leave for work.

☆

You've sent fan mail to a fishing lure.

You Might Be a Redneck If . . .

Your flashlight holds more
than four batteries.

You Might Be a Redneck If . . .

Your hood ornament is a duck decoy.

☆

You've spent more than half a day in a fishing shop.

☆

There is a ham hanging from your front porch.

☆

You've ever gone hunting on a tractor.

☆

Your dog rides in the front seat
and your kids ride in the back.

☆

Your favorite cologne is Deep Woods Off.

You Might Be a Redneck If . . .

You traded your truck for a dog.

☆

You were baptized on a boat ramp.

☆

Your birdhouse used to be a Clorox bottle.

☆

You have an aboveground swimming pool
that you fish out of.

☆

Your Fourth of July fireworks were flea bombs.

☆

You think *Silence of the Lambs* is what happens
when somebody walks toward the barn.

All you see in your
rearview mirror is dogs.

You've ever eaten out of a minnow bucket.

☆

Every "Deer Crossing" sign on your road
is shot full of holes.

You Might Be a Redneck If . . .

Your hunting dog fetches more beer than birds.

☆

You've ever shot a partridge out of a pear tree.

☆

Your wading boots double as dress pants.

☆

When you talk about great mullet fishermen,
Granny's name always comes up.

☆

Your license plate frame mentions fishing.

☆

You actually know which kinds of leaves
make the best substitute for toilet paper.

You Might Be a Redneck If . . .

You think megabytes means a good day of fishing.

You Might Be a Redneck If . . .

Your dream home is a bass boat.

☆

You've ever named a child for a good dog.

☆

There is an electronic singing fish
in more than three rooms of your house.

☆

Your knife is sharper than you are.

☆

Your idea of a fun night out
is chasing dogs through a swamp.

☆

You saw Rock City and said, "Now I can die!"